Mosaic Genius

Mosaic Genius

*Building Beautiful Things
with Broken Pieces*

Christal M. Jackson, BA, MTS

White River Press

Amherst, Massachusetts

MOSAIC GENIUS
Copyright © 2019 by Christal M. Jackson.

First published 2019 by White River Press, PO Box 3561, Amherst, Massachusetts 01004

ISBN: 978-1-887043-51-9

Front cover image: "Brilliance" Copyright 2006 Synthia SAINT JAMES (www.SynthiaSAINTJAMES.com). Used with permission.

Author photo credit: Al Torres, altorresphotography.com

Library of Congress Cataloging-in-Publication Data on file with the publisher

Acknowledgements

I want to thank Linda Roghaar for coaching me through writing this book for nearly ten years. She believed in my story and ability long before I did. I'm deeply grateful that God gave me such a gift.

Thank you also to Jean Stone, the editor extraordinaire whose ability to listen with her head and heart helped me tell this story. Your trustworthiness with intricate details and deeply personal thoughts have helped me share.

And thanks to my Spelman Sisters—Aleesha Taylor (the first person to read the manuscript), Lybra Clemons, and Spring Taylor for being the epitome of sisters on this journey. For every time you let me sleep on your sofa, for being sounding boards and cheerleaders, your support has been invaluable.

Thanks also to:

Celeste Smith for holding my vision safe and opening yourself and your family to support my work, I can't thank you enough;

Yolanda Caraway for opening doors, opening your home, and encouragement when I needed it the most;

Charisse Lillie for your affirmation and support from day one that has given me such courage;

Stephanie Bell-Rose for being my biggest champion, walking me through doors and encouraging me;

Melissa Bradley for being an amazing big sister, who has always said "yes," and whose wife and children shared you with me, for which I am so grateful;

The late David Deveuax for ALWAYS willing to help me find a way to explore the intersection of vocation and calling even when it looked different.

Jamal Harrison Bryant for recognizing my genius long before I did and for every effort to open any and every door on my behalf.

Erik Moore thank you for being the perfectly imperfect mirror of grief on the journey towards wholeness.

Lastly, to my family for supporting everything I've ever wanted to do . . . THANK YOU!

Dedication

To my great-grandfather Arthur Jackson Sr. and my grandfather Arthur Jackson Jr. for preparing a place for me. You planned for me before I was born.

Leslie Bowie Wells Brooks, the best big sister ever!
May 6, 1967–November 4, 2008

CONTENTS

—Section I—

Purpose

Heartbreak

MY PERSONAL JOURNEY OF TRANSFORMATION

It happened about twenty-five minutes after Barack Obama had been declared the forty-fourth president of the United States. I was lying across a chair watching the election results with my mom at my parents' home in Fort Bend County, Texas. I know we were both thinking, *Wow. A black man and woman with two little black girls were going to occupy the White House. Unbelievable.*

Then my phone rang. I answered the call; the conversation went a bit like this: "Christal, she's gone."

I closed my eyes. "Who was with her?"

"Her mom."

"Did she say anything?"

"No."

"Was it peaceful?"

"Very. Her mom told her that Barack Obama won, and she said: 'Awesome.' Then she took her last breath."

I declined the offer to go and see her because I had been given the ultimate gift of saying goodbye less than forty-eight hours ago. And now, my friend Leslie had transitioned from being my big sister to becoming my guardian angel.

I cried. I turned to my mom who instinctually knew what had happened. "You will see her again," she said.

I thought: *Perhaps. But she's not here right now, and none of those things we talked about doing together will ever happen.*

When my phone began to buzz with calls from people who no doubt wanted to share the excitement about our new president, I went to bed. History was being made, but I was feeling lost and confused. Isn't life funny, how so many different things—things that yank our feelings in opposite directions—can, and do, happen in the world at the same time?

The week leading up to Leslie's funeral is a bit of a blur, but I remember I had a chance to spend some time with her daughter, Sesily. A sweet tea party with a two-year-old is a perfect remedy for any heartache, but ours made my heart hurt even more because I knew that Sesily would never know her beautiful mother in the way I wanted. I wanted her to be able to hear her mother's voice, see her smile, experience her laughter, learn from her wisdom, admire her courage and creativity, marvel at her beauty, and model her humility and grace. Instead, she would only have stories, photos, and videos. I thought: *God this is just not right.* During that time, I was angry and hurt, and I had strong words of displeasure for God. I was upset because it did not seem fair. At one point, when I was driving down the street, a nasty driver cut me off. I shouted, "No! Why are you still alive?" After all, he was a mean person, and my friend had been so nice.

Leslie was my role model. She was from Houston like me, a product of public school like me, and loved Texas hair. She agreed with me that there was nothing like a roller set on a Friday! We both liked Houston food, crafts, and sparkly things; we loved our families and cherished our friends. Both of our brothers were pastors; our moms were our best friends; and we both went to Spelman and lived in the same fresh(wo)man dorm room—Packard 112. We loved plays, and loved to entertain, but each of us appreciated being alone. She was an entrepreneur; I was toying with the idea. The confidence she had in my ability gave me the courage to make the big leap. Leslie was also my angel investor.

One day, I shared my idea with her. I described what my business would look like, the ways in which it could grow, the good works it could do by helping others. She asked me how I planned to start it. I explained that my first order of business was to have an event—a learning, working opportunity for others to see how we could each help make the world a better place. She listened attentively, thought for a moment, then said: "I want to pay for your first event."

"No," I replied. "I'm not going to take your money." At the time, she was already sick; there was no way I was going to let her pay for my dream.

But as the days went by she would casually ask, "When are you going to start?" She continued to try and give me money, and I continued to refuse. Then, after a couple of weeks had passed, I found a check in my bag. I knew she would not take it back.

Before Leslie died, I officially launched my consulting business. I remember that morning as if it were yesterday. I was so nervous! I was in my apartment in the Galleria/Uptown Park area of Houston, pacing the floor, when my phone rang. It was Leslie. "Are you nervous?" she asked.

"Yes."

"Don't be. It's going to be just fine."

"Okay, then let me finish getting dressed. I'll see you there."

A few minutes later the phone rang again. And, again, it was Leslie. "Always remember that you are the expert," she said. "People will come to you because they need your advice and your knowledge."

Taking a deep breath, I felt like I grew a few feet taller. "Okay," I answered. "Okay." I finished dressing and headed out the door with a bit of a hop in my step that hadn't been there before.

I had launched a business that was centered on different types of heartbreak, but the irony was that the person who had helped me get started was now gone, and my own heart was broken. She had been immensely instrumental in my own journey toward wholeness, and suddenly I needed to apply all that I'd learned from her to my inner self, as well as to my work.

One of the ways I coped with her death was to work. Whenever I met with a new client, I asked him or her to articulate to me what broke/breaks their heart. The question often threw people for a loop, but then they would look at me—often with tears in their eyes—amazed that, for the first time, they were able to connect their own, personal experience to something so meaningful.

When I speak of heartbreak, these are the things that hurt my heart the most:

- **Racism**, especially institutional racism, because it has been justified as policy, and it has been legalized. My biological grandmother died when my mother was twelve years old from something that could possibly have been treated if she'd been allowed to go to the *white* hospital. But she was not. Instead, she had to go to the *black* hospital, where the equipment and care were not equitable. I'm certain that to white people who created those policies it didn't matter that children would lose parents, people would lose spouses, and grandchildren would lose grandparents. Apparently, the thought was that black people shouldn't receive good medical treatment because they didn't deserve to be treated like humans. My mother had been blessed with two aunts who raised her, which was even more important to her when, a few months after she lost her mother, her father died. I never knew my grandmother, but the aunts who raised my mother, my great-aunts, took on the role of grandmother to me. They were wonderful.

Institutional racism is far more dangerous than crazy people running around throwing out racial slurs. I was five years old the first time I was called a nigger. A little boy did it—his father stood by and laughed. I told my brothers, who told me what to say if anyone did that to me again. Unfortunately, someone did, but that time it was an adult, a woman. I hurled some colorful words right back at her across a counter. She looked stunned; I smiled. Today, I wish that shouting matches and name-calling could fix poor healthcare, poor education, and provide access to capital. Sadly, they don't.

- **Abuse** breaks my heart. I don't know what's worse: physical abuse or abuse of power. I grew up watching women flee domestic violence at the hands of their spouses. Our home was a safe haven for women a few times, and it was confusing to me. I remember waking up, sharing my bed with a woman or children, and I immediately knew that something bad had happened to them the night before. My mother would tell me what I needed to know about the situation, but I knew not to ask any more questions. I knew that whatever the details were didn't matter, only that the people had to move in the night, and that they wore their clothes, not their pajamas like I did.

It was clear something was wrong. And that was enough for me.

Abuse of power also disturbs me. I'm convinced that I took a sabbatical from going to church because the absolute abuse of power and authority in the church was the worst thing I'd ever witnessed. I believe there is a special place in hell for people who take advantage of people when they look to them for help. Especially when they are vulnerable. This is why I believe that children, seniors, and the disabled should be in a protected class. Abuse of power has led to so much destruction of people, visions, businesses, organizations, and the list goes on and on. For example, every time I hear about a black inventor never having received recognition or being robbed because he or she was basically not in the seat of power, my blood boils. I had the privilege of being a part of the Woodhull Institute for Ethical Leadership, the focus of which was on the ethical use of power. Those principles have helped me be the type of leader that I wanted to be.

- **Poverty** breaks my heart. My mother's friend tells a story of how, when I was preschool age, I realized what being poor looked like. I had seen something on television, and it had scared me: being poor meant you had no food, no toys, no car. I knew I didn't want to live like that; the thought of poverty literally scared me. As I look around our world today, I wish more people were disturbed at the sight of poor people, but, instead, they have learned how not to see them. I grew up in an average middle class black family, but I worry about families now, about how they will have to accomplish a lot more than what my parents were able to accomplish, just to be considered *middle class.*

Economic vulnerability and inequity makes me cry the same way it did when I was that young preschool girl. Now, I cry even more because I've seen what real wealth looks like, and because the gap in this country has become horrifying. On any given day, I can have a conversation with representatives from an organization who would do anything to receive $10,000; a few hours later I can have a conversation with a group that will decline one million dollars for all sorts of reasons ranging from *brand dilution* to *lack of alignment.*

I go to sleep every night burdened by the fact that some child who probably lives not far from me must endure the horrors of poverty. And it's not only children. Our seniors are just as vulnerable and are often left to choose between buying food or medicine. I have to work really hard not to fall into a slump of guilt because that isn't healthy and people don't need guilt—they need equity and, above all, opportunity.

Recovery

HOW SELF-DISCOVERY HAS BEEN
CRITICAL TO PURSUING MY PURPOSE

I remember sitting in Sunday School as a child, listening to my teacher talk about Noah and the Ark, the great flood, and rainbows. I have always loved rainbows because I believe they are God's gift to us after a storm. When I was a Girl Scout, a drawing of a rainbow that I did earned me first place in a competition. It was bold and beautiful, the way we often feel after we've survived a personal storm.

Losing Leslie at a critical period in my life made it even more complicated for me to handle her death. Early on, I had prepared myself for a career that would allow me to serve people, especially the most vulnerable, but I sought to accomplish this through a very traditional space for the black community—the church. But even before I was accepted into Duke Divinity School, I knew I didn't want to go. Typically, when one chooses a career path, there is someone who serves as a model for that career and the life that can evolve from it. While I had met many wonderful people, women in particular, who had become religious professionals, I knew that by the time I was fifty, I would not want my career and my life to look like theirs. As I matriculated at Duke, I was even more convinced that this was not the right path for me. But because I'd been raised to finish what I started, I finished. Through it all, I was miserable. I never saw my education as a tool for transformation. Yes, I believe in theological training, but I learned that anyone who is committed to service should probably pursue another form of training—one that can better equip him or her to meet the real challenges and day-to-day realities that our communities face. I believe we need more scientists, innovators, researchers, and social entrepreneurs and fewer people who are simply great at delivering speeches—including some social impact celebrities. As the old saying goes, talk is cheap. We need more substance that is truly representative of real life.

About a decade ago, I had no one to whom I could articulate this concept except my friend Leslie, who happened to be both very Christian and black. When I tried to broach the conversation with others—both peers and elders—I was often met with the same advice: that I needed to pray because I must be going through some type of crisis. In other words, I must be lost. When one person actually used those words, I remember I sat there thinking, "No, you are the one who's lost, because this institution thinks it has been focused on service but has, instead, been damaged by people who think the way you do, who cannot see the bigger, broader picture."

For nearly five years after my formal education, I knew that I loved God and respected the church, but I also knew that a traditional religious career path would not be right for me. Still, I dressed up on Sunday mornings as if I were going to church but I would, instead, go to the movies and sit in the center of a practically empty theater. When the movie was over, I'd leave and head home. What I later discovered is that a big part of recovery happens in isolation—whether someone is praying, pondering, or sitting in an empty theater. Now that I have a healthier sense of what the modern day church can and can't provide for our communities, my expectations have adjusted to value it even with its limitations.

Today, after working in the social impact sector for nearly twenty years, I recognize that within the existing ecosystem there are major limitations for impact on black and brown communities. Why? Because the system has been designed and operates mostly by a few privileged whites. Subsequently, most of the interventions are not effective and soon run their course, resulting in little noticeable impact compared to the investment. In addition, a few handpicked black social impact leaders have discovered a "hustle," and the fire they might have initially had to be true servants has turned them into puppets for dollars from a few sources. Much like within the church, there is a strong possibility that the blacks within the sector will transfer those same bad habits into the sector and that, once again, vulnerable people will pay the price. I've learned that people are people and they are going to be people. Does this mean I have lowered my expectations? No. I have merely adjusted them.

We've all lost something or someone. There is a process we must go through in order to move forward; or we can stay stuck and create an alternative universe, which I don't recommend. I lost something when I had to learn to insult white people back after they'd insulted me; I lost something when I woke up next to a woman running from an abusive husband; I lost something every time I witnessed first-hand accounts of people trapped in endless cycles of poverty that they can't escape; and I lost something November 4, 2008, the day that Leslie died. But I believe that for every loss there is recovery.

Recovery enables us to discover a few important things:

- **Release control**. In the early 2000s, when I was at the height of my career transition, I was in a car accident. While I was at the hospital being tended to by a nurse before a doctor came in, the nurse measured my blood pressure and said, "You sure are calm." She took it several more times and finally said, "Excellent." I was lying there thinking, *Why wouldn't I be calm*? I had, after all, survived the accident. I had survived the storm, so it was time to relax and breathe. I was on the other side of it; all was good. The storm hadn't killed me.
- **Trust the process**. I love it when I meet people who decide they want to write a book or start a non-profit and expect that things will take off like

a rocket. Even if they do achieve what might look like "overnight success," it didn't happen quite that way: they must have established a process that got them there. After I created the idea of Head and Heart Philanthropy, it was six years before I shared it with someone, because, until then, I wasn't sure that it made total sense. Then, while in New York at JP Morgan having coffee with a private banker, I told her my idea: I trusted her enough to share it. She responded by saying, "That's an excellent idea. And a necessary one." That was all I needed. It had taken me six years to tell someone, but during that time I was researching, planning, formulating, thinking, and re-thinking. And re-thinking some more. In other words, I was following a process. It did not happen in a flash.

A good idea takes time, and once I wrapped my head around that, I knew I would be fine. After all, every job I'd ever had had equipped me to run a social impact agency. I had started as an intern and worked my way up, around, and into the sector. I invested just about every extra dollar I had into educational opportunities that would help me find out more about it. In order to learn the *science* of social impact—and, yes, there definitely is a science—I did work that I would have otherwise considered was "beneath" me, including entry level positions from clerical to process monitoring, which basically included monitoring and tracking grants. I didn't care about having a title: I only wanted to learn every possible facet about the work. Also, because my academic training was in a different field, I had to find a way to acquire new skills and make new friends. I didn't know the "language" of the social impact world, so I had to network, network, network. I also learned the importance of respecting the process, and to be cautious of others who might want to cut in line because they can't survive the hard stuff. This field, like many, requires a lot of hard work.

- **Stay focused**. I've heard so many things about the importance of having *balance* in life, yet every successful entrepreneur knows that they work almost all the time. Even when they're not actually *at* work, they are most often thinking or talking about some aspect of their work. So, long ago, I gave up on the idea of having balance; instead, I believe in the power of *focus*. Here are a few simple things I do to achieve—and maintain—focus:

- I use *electronics* to my advantage! I have my cell phone set to tell me when to wake up and when to go to sleep. I love the sounds for each: chirping birds to wake me; a gentle ocean surf to lull me into sleep. At sunset, and when possible, I watch a cooking show or do latch hook for relaxation.

- I have an incredible *scheduler* and a very small, close-knit inner circle. According to my schedule, I focus on work, but I manage to include time for my friends and loved ones, too. Because I am more focused, I have learned to include all the people and events that matter to me. I'm not interested in being at everything. I remember that when I first moved to New York, my friends told me the places I *had* to be—when and where and how. I smiled, but I knew there was no way in the world I was going to live like that. I knew that I was going to have to focus and to set my intentions on what made sense for me at that stage of my life. That was where I wanted to be, so that was what I focused on.

- I have a set of *core values* that I try to base my life and work around; those values have become the foundation of my focus. If anything contradicts them, it's a distraction, and it's not for me. Every day, distractions are all around. I am able to keep them to a minimum by sticking to my core values.

- Another way I stay focused is through my commitment to *self care*. Every year, I give myself the luxury of a silent retreat. Also, I use the early mornings to be quiet; I cherish the daily gift of waking up and being able to hear myself breathe. To anyone who has ever watched a person take his or her last breath, this act has brand new meaning. Wherever I live, birds seem to find me; they sing no matter what. To hear their songs outside my window is another gift. On a great day, I get to watch the sunrise. These daily miracles carry me forward and help me set my focus and intention for the day. They are simple reminders that I did not create my life, that I am blessed to be alive, and that nature—with its cheery birds and rising sun—knows how to respond to everything around us by doing what it was created to do. I try to translate that into my own life as I move onward through recovery.

There is something about being in a safe place and in safe conversations that allows innovative thought to flourish and relationships to be built. Head and Heart Philanthropy focuses on creating that space and is unapologetic about creating that space specifically for people of color. And, our communities desperately need us to be thinking and acting together with a sense of urgency, bringing together ideas and capital to make them happen.

—Lisa Nutter

—Section II—

Community

Moments Turned into Movements

HOW AMERICA'S BIGGEST MOMENTS OF TRANSFORMATION WERE SPARKED BY MOMENTS

While attending the annual *Leading Women Defined* conference hosted by BET Networks, I had the pleasure of hearing Sybrina Fulton speak. As she spoke, many of us sat around the table asking, "How does she do it?"

For those who might have been under a rock, Sybrina Fulton is the mother of Trayvon Martin—a Florida teen who was shot and killed by a community patrolman, George Zimmerman. Trayvon was carrying a bag of Skittles and an Arizona Iced Tea, which sounds quite harmless. To make matters worse, George Zimmerman was not charged with a crime, but rather he walked away a free man because of Florida's stand-your-ground law. Like many who had tuned in to watch the trial, I had had some concerns about how this would play out. When the verdict was read, I wasn't surprised, but I was deeply disappointed.

I was disappointed because the first black president would have to address the modern day Emmett Till narrative—the 14-year old boy lynched in Mississippi in 1955 after being falsely accused of flirting with a white woman.

I was disappointed because racial bias was clouding judgment again.

I was disappointed because, like many, I would have to look at black male children who we love, and acknowledge that deep down in our guts we can't protect them.

That night I wept for Sybrina and Tracey because their baby, Trayvon, was dead and seemingly it didn't matter. I wept tears of anger and went to sleep and, the next day, I started all over again.

Fast forward to 2017 in a ballroom at the St. Regis Bal Harbour. A strong woman—Sybrina—was speaking about channeling the pain from the moment of her son's death into a movement. I had seen her before, at a Congressional Black Caucus (CBC) event for women in Washington D.C. That time, I had been sad and embarrassed and could only hug her. This time it was different; it was different because she had found purpose in pain. If she could do that, then I knew that my job was going to be to help her.

Throughout time, the history of this country will be accented by moments that strong women turned into movements. It was Soujourner Truth who, as a former slave, first addressed civil rights in 1851 at the Ohio Women's Convention. It was Rosa Parks who, in 1955, was credited for accelerating the civil rights movement after being forced to give up her seat on a public bus after she'd worked all day. Two years later, it was Daisy Bates, then president of the NAACP Arkansas chapter, who, after the Supreme Court's decision that school segregation was unconstitutional had gone unenforced, initiated the first successful school integration at Little Rock. And this list goes on and on. While each of these movements had different points of origin they share similar principles that lead to impact.

Resolve

When we remain stuck in the ugliness of a moment, not only is it harmful to you, but it also disempowers you to help others. Take back your strength and your sober judgment, and grab some grace so you can move forward. Start today with the drive and focus on addressing the issue.

Evolve

Moments seem small but they change us. Guess what? We're supposed to change. We're supposed to exist in each other's space. That's what makes the work of social impact so special because it enables us to get into each other's spaces—and out of the ones that we occupy. Our old habits and thoughts are challenged, and we emerge as new people. This process isn't comfortable, but it is necessary.

Act

I love the saying, *Rome wasn't built in a day*. Give yourself permission to build the plane as you fly it. It's okay to not know all the steps in between, but you must make an effort. Understand that where you start will not look much at all like where you will end. As you gain momentum you will attract the partners and relationships you need to move you along. It all begins with a first act.

What about YOU? Is there a single moment that profoundly shaped the trajectory of your personal life or career? Have you begun to move forward, or are you stuck? Only you can truly answer that question. It is deeply personal. But regardless of the answer, understand that, in the grand scheme of things, a moment is just that. If it speaks to you, listen. Resolve, evolve, and act.

Where were you when . . . is typically the start of what will likely become an interesting and provocative conversation.

I remember hearing Martin Luther King's sister, Christine King Farris, describe where she was when she found out that her brother had been assassinated. She remembered it as if it were yesterday, not decades earlier. (I won't share her comments in this book because it wasn't a speech but a conversation.)

I also remember where I was during some very historical moments that held special meaning for me, including the shooting death of Marvin Gaye in 1984; when Mickey Leland was in a plane crash and declared dead in 1989; the horror of September 11, 2001; when the Space Shuttle Columbia blew up over Texas and Louisiana in 2003; and, more recently, when I first saw a self-driving vehicle.

I also remember when I was no longer afraid. Yes, free of fear, failure, rejection, messing up, being alone, or all of the stuff that keeps us from being our best self, living our most complete life. I suffered a life-changing injury as a child and have had to live with the implications of that injury since. When I was younger, I sort of understood what it meant, but my mother shielded me from knowing too much about what was really going on. As good mothers do, they tell their children what they need to know, only when they need to know it. Otherwise, I would have lived in my head and ultimately allowed the injury to paralyze me. Instead, that experience has been the root of my deep compassion for people—whether they are at their best or their worst. I try very hard not to judge people on what I call their worst day, because I don't want to be judged when I'm on mine. I always hope that people will take the sum of our days and decide who and what we most deserve.

Moments are incredibly impressionable, which is why I try to be very careful about how I treat people and, just as importantly, how I allow them to treat me. A moment, after all, has the capacity to shift the entire trajectory of your life. That's why I believe in doing this work. There is something that all of us can do. As much as we talk about the business of social impact, the *heart* of the work is much more important. I named my agency

Head and Heart Philanthropy because you can't have one without the other—not for social impact to be truly effective. This work is hard and very process oriented, it's not in and out, fly by the cuff, based on real time, but rather, you must think of it in terms of a longitudinal study, long term. There is the pre-work, the process, the evaluation, and then course correction if and when necessary. Trust me—course correction is common and often essential.

So what can people do when they care but don't know where to start? Glad you asked.

1. **Start with what you care about**. Do you even know what you really care about? Think about *the things you complain most about,* things that you feel are broken and need to be fixed. Narrow those things down to a single thing you can focus on. For instance, maybe you don't like the public school in your neighborhood. What don't you like about it? Is it the landscape, the paint, the marquee, the library, or the absence of a computer lab? You might be inclined to choose two, three, or a dozen things that you'd like to see changed, but at this point, it's important to focus on one. This will ensure a greater chance for success, and will help get you started so, if you want, you can move on to other items in the future.

2. **List your personal resources**. Now that you've identified what you don't like, it's time

to think about your friends. They can, after all, be your most successful allies in helping you determine a jumping-off point. Start with your inner circle, usually your friends or acquaintances. Don't leave anyone off the list because you don't think they'd "be interested!" If you know them, and they know you, write down their names. They're already your friends, so chances are, you have things in common. They probably have a mindset that's similar to yours, so they will want to hear what you're working on. Next, think about your outer circle, those "friends of friends" that you've met on occasion—even if the occasion was only once. Think of it as if you are launching a book club and you invite your friends that you know enjoy reading, and they invite their friends that enjoy reading, and they invite their friends, and . . . you get the picture. By the time you look up, you might have started with one person, but now you likely have twenty. Maybe more!

3. **Assess the strengths and capacity of your circle.** Set people up to win. After they fully understand your long-range goals, ask them to take on an aspect that *they know how to do well,* not what they *aspire* to do well. No role is too small, but a role can be too big. Don't kill yourself; don't kill the members of your circle. This is a marathon, not a sprint.

4. **Create a plan of action.** Treat your project as if it embodies a real workplace with goals that are **SMART**: **S**pecific, **M**easurable, **A**ttainable, **R**ealistic, and **T**imely. If your project doesn't align with all of these, you might be setting yourself up for lots of frustration, time lost, and, ultimately, disappointment. But following these simple steps will get you where you want to be and create the positive social impact you envision.

5. **Focus and get started!** I cannot stress enough the importance of focus. No matter what any of us want, the truth is, none of us can fix the whole world. But we can move forward and fix our little corner . . ., which can evolve into a bigger corner . . . then a bigger one. By starting with *focus*, the results might take you in an exciting new direction that turns out to be greater and more meaningful than you ever imagined. You never know until you begin!

The Not-So-New America

WHY THE WORK OF SOCIAL IMPACT IS SO IMPORTANT.

When I was 4 years old, my first playmate was Miss Ollie. She was 92. Little did I know that my journey into social impact started as I sat on the floor with her, coloring together, playing with our dolls, helping one another put our hair in pigtails.

I consider myself to be very blessed. Today, I get to earn a living by seeing people at their best—people who typically want to fix the world or at least the brokenness that they know in the world. Understanding that brokenness is relative: it is based on one's personal ethos.

My mother was a nurse. Throughout her early career, she worked at various residence and nursing homes throughout the Jackson, Mississippi and Houston, Texas area. It wasn't long before she became disturbed by the way our country's seniors were being treated: she saw them often poorly fed and clothed, frequently without good hygiene, with little positive daily interaction, and a whole lot of just plain being ignored. For whatever reasons—lack of funding, under staffing, unawareness—it was as if the phrase "quality of life" had not yet been coined. My mother recognized that the patients were being minimized as human beings. So she quit her job and started her own nursing home.

It wasn't easy for her. However, that didn't stop my mom. By the time she was 13 she had lost both of her parents and was subsequently raised by her eldest sisters and their spouses. I'm forever indebted to them for loving my mom. The women were very different but shared the same values around education, faith, work, and family. I see both of them in me.

My friend Miss Ollie was neither a relative nor a neighbor lady who sometimes stopped by to see me. She was a patient at my mother's nursing home who suffered from dementia, who became part of our caring family made up of total strangers.

I remember being struck by the facts that the residents never had visitors or that no one came to celebrate their birthday. My young brain didn't quite know what to make of this. So after peppering my mom with questions about it, she told me they were wards of the state, they had no one, so we had to take care of them. I was sad then, and, many years later, I am still sad at the mere thought that people can be thrown away. But from that day on, I started helping. I was probably in the way more often than not, but they let me help. I set the table at mealtime, prepared bath water "'cause they needed bubbles," helped put lotion on their hands and feet, and sang them songs. I loved when they would smile. They called me Miss Chris, and I addressed them with the same level of respect. They were a part of me.

During that time, my mother was fortunate to have help with my brothers and me, help that gave her time that allowed her to establish and run the home. My father was supportive; the aides shuttled my brothers and me around when my parents weren't available. My mom had no problem getting patients: the social workers felt good about placing people with us. However, scaling to enable strategic business growth was a challenge for her. I'm certain her margins were small because she cared for the residents as if they were her own. I remember many nights sitting around the dinner table with them, sharing the meal. I also remember that when the staff wasn't able to get there, I spent the day, and sometimes the night, at work with my mom.

Eventually, because my dad had better opportunities, we moved back to Houston, and my mom turned patients over to other caregivers. She had planned to start back up in Houston, but after being swindled out of her money, she needed a job that she could count on. Also, as life went on, our needs increased. She never opened another home.

Through it all, my mother was not only my role model but also my mentor. And though I had no desire to become a nurse, I knew I needed to help others, to try and make the world a better place in an arena that could serve many.

That has been my ethos, my passion. My greatest reward is that I now get to help others find theirs. And together we get to witness the best of humanity. I think Miss Ollie would be pleased.

Development of Personal Ethos

1. Personal Discovery—*Start Where You Are with What You Have.*

This is probably the most difficult part of the process. The world is so noisy that determining where to start can be hard.

I thought about my first year at Spelman. Leslie—my friend since childhood who became my college roommate—used to laugh at me as I changed my major every other day. Back then, I thought that I would make a career out of working in the church because helping people is what's most important to me. Unfortunately, that's not the primary focus of church. That journey left me deeply disappointed and scarred, but ultimately it set the stage for my purpose and work. Five-year-old Christal is now the adult Christal, creating safe spaces for the vulnerable.

2. Find Your Passion—*Be Unapologetic!*

For the first three years I was in business, I didn't make any money; my amazing parents and my aunt (my father's sister) supported me. I learned lots of discipline, and even now I still function most of the time as if I'm not making a dime. When I'm on business travel, I stay near the airport at a place with a gym and a free airport shuttle. I travel in economy class, using first class only when I'm upgraded. I can live out of a carry-on for a week. I've slept in an airport, not in a lounge, and thought nothing of it because I was focused. I'm driven because too many black and brown people are not safe.

3. Focus—*Choose Something and Stick to It!*

When I was a grant writer, I didn't understand why the directives were so specific. It was so frustrating when they wouldn't abandon an idea or path, when they were so restrictive about business plans and goals. But, huh, now I get it. You must choose a concrete idea, practice, or concept, or time will pass and you will look up and not have accomplished anything. As a person, with a big heart, I have to say, "No" a lot, otherwise, I'd be deeply engaged in a bunch of stuff, and I'd become distracted.

4. Watch the Results/Impact

I've learned patience and the benefit of delayed gratification. I wish that I could say it was the result of fun and happy experiences; it wasn't. It was from sitting with loved ones as they waited while facing the end of life; it was from numerous personal sacrifices, from delaying starting a family, from not accepting certain jobs and clients. And, I have no regrets. Every time a person tells me that, after leaving a convening that I've hosted, he or she has adopted my strategy recommendations, and/or invested in, or with, a black or brown person, I feel the same joy I felt when playing dolls with Miss Ollie: We are all just people; we must be there for one another.

Using History as a Roadmap for the Future

SOLUTIONS TO COMPLICATED SOCIAL ISSUES AND A LOOK AT MODELS OF SUCCESS

I've been radicalized since before kindergarten. The first time I was called a nigger, I hadn't even begun a formal education. I hadn't slept on my first mat at naptime with my favorite blanket (which, by the way, I still have and it's just like new). I hadn't even lost my baby teeth or fully learned how to ride a bike without training wheels. And I was born in the 1970s to parents who were at least three generations from slavery.

It happened on a usual day at the gas station. My dad didn't allow me to get out of the car as he pumped the gas, but he always let my window down and I could talk to him while he pumped it. At that age, I loved to talk to anyone who would hold a conversation. So I chatted it up with him as he pumped. In the car across from us was a father and his son. The little boy looked about my age. Because I was friendly, the way I had been taught to be, I waved and said, "Hello." He replied with, "You nigger."

I was stunned. I was also confused because I could tell it wasn't a term of endearment nor was it friendly.

After he called me a nigger, he looked to his father and they both smiled.

My father didn't say anything to the boy but told the father, "You shouldn't teach your son to be ugly."

I couldn't wait to get home to tell my brothers what had happened. I remember bursting into their room and blurting out the news. They sat me down and gave me some advice that had somehow helped them when faced with being called that hateful word—it was a list of slurs. They said I should use them the next time a white person called me such a thing.

Well surely, it happened again. But that time, I was ready. I hurled my brothers' words back to an adult. Her face turned red—I suppose that she was shocked.

At that very early age, I then knew that I wanted to live in a black neighborhood, go to a black school, and attend a black church so I wouldn't have to deal with white people calling me that name. Thankfully my parents made all of that happen for us. My siblings and I were comfortable and protected from the reality of having to explain—or feel "less than" for—being black. To take it even further, all of my doctors and even my parents' accountant were black. I now know how hard it was for my parents to create that safe and protected world for us, and I am deeply grateful.

The flip side of the coin, however, was I was very uncomfortable with white people for a very long time. When they were nice, I questioned what they must want or why. I would never be caught alone with a white person for fear of them accusing me of something and me being left defenseless.

I remember the first time a white person tried to offer me control over a checking account at work. I refused. I asked her to manage the money and sign all checks. I remember being asked was I uncomfortable with money. I replied, "No, but I'm uncomfortable with your money."

I also remember I would never be caught in an elevator with all white men, much like the way many white women wouldn't be caught in an elevator with all black men. Thankfully, though, I've met some white men that I will let give me a hug, which is a long way from refusing an elevator ride. I will now spend the night in the home of white person, drive their cars, and eat their food. This behavior would have been unimaginable to my late grandmothers.

Some might read this and think, "My goodness, she's paranoid or racist." But I was merely conditioned by my reality.

What had seemed like innocent name calling at a gas station wound up shaping me in ways that I could never have imagined. The issue of race is so complex, and I'm only willing to discuss it with people who are willing to admit the truth about the ways in which we have been radicalized in this country and abroad.

Post-Obama

I always had a weird feeling about this country electing "a black man" as president. I sensed that black people would fall in love with the symbol, and that, eventually, white people would hate it. Therefore, a Trump presidency is not a shock to me. In fact, I totally understand it. It makes sense that it would follow what some had come to think was a tragic mistake or freak accident—a black family in the White House. I understand why white people feel like they have lost their country and want it back. I'm certain that little boy I encountered at the gas station has become a Trump supporter, unless something really drastic had happened in his life.

Race is a complicated conversation, because in order to truly discuss the implications of it, we must discuss its origins and the fact that racism is built on sustaining a system of power: it is, therefore, systemic.

As much as I enjoy working in the social impact sector, I hate it. It's so annoying at times, just utterly ridiculous, especially when people try to deal with race. There are several well intentioned (I guess) models we can point to that infiltrated low-moderate income black and brown communities with promises to help improve educational and health outcomes for communities of color. But their intentions went awry. Instead of helping, they have done a great deal of damage and wasted a lot of money because they didn't treat the people they were serving as equals but rather objects they were "saving" or "fixing." Rather than looking at the system, they addressed the symptoms.

So I'm leery of organizations with predominately white boards and a few happy black people on staff with titles but no real influence, and with all-white donors and white founders fixing problems for black and brown people. It's always a train wreck waiting to happen. But I understand why black and brown people with influence and resources don't collaborate: they don't want to spend their energy trying to jump through hoops to help their own when they can use that same energy to just serve their communities.

Earlier we described how impactful moments can be. Most of what we care about is birthed out of hearts, but the models are typically birthed out of our heads. It's the analytical work that forces us to take SMART goals and create something scalable or sustainable. I'm generous by nature, yet frugal. This is likely due to the fact that I'm the daughter of an entrepreneur, and we understand very well that it can be feast or famine, so you learn to always stay somewhere in between. Now that I'm older and my federal reserve bank-parents and aunt are older, I'm definitely more frugal.

To add another layer, I now live in the Bay Area surrounded by venture capitalists and founders of all types of companies and organizations. My early life experience helps me blend in very well with the culture. But social entrepreneurs are a different breed of business leader. There is the understanding that you want to solve a problem, but that you also have to make money. Sometimes mixing the two is difficult. In a capitalistic society, this becomes a very delicate balance. Which is why when, as a do-gooder, you set out to do good, it's very important that you understand the culture of those you intend to help.

First generation programs founded by non-first generations often miss the mark because as much as the intent is good, the execution may be a bit off. For example, I was talking to a first generation college student one day, and she politely corrected me on a few comments I'd made about the need to encourage students. She said, "Encouragement is nice, but if you've never seen an example, you might be inspired, but you are still ill-equipped." It was a "light bulb moment" for me. Some of my frustration over big machine nonprofits that swoop into black and brown communities, grab black talent, and target first generationers without being culturally appropriate or sensitive was being reflected in my own ignorance. To put it plainly, I wasn't using my head. I was speaking out of turn rather than listening. Successful models work because people didn't lead only with their heads but also with their hearts.

So I searched out a few successful venture capitalists, spent some time with them, and found out what it took to build a successful sustainable company.

So, what does it take to run a successful nonprofit? I sat down with Kimberly Bryant, founder and CEO of Black Girls Code to learn a bit about those things that she feels contribute to her organization's success. Kimberly has certainly walked the walk and talked the talk. As a freshman in college and an electrical engineering major, Kimberly was captivated by the evolving languages of computer programming. Years later, she realized the absence of African-American women in the field: her answer was to launch Black Girls Code. Today, having partnered with leading technology and communications corporations, the organization works to empower girls from 7–17 to enter the STEM fields and become leaders in computer science and technology. An article in *Forbes* about Black Girls Code even predicted that "The Next Steve Jobs will be a Woman of Color."

As to her success, Kimberly told me that the ingredients of a successful nonprofit aren't much different from those of a for-profit company, but the stakeholders are looking for something a bit different. She explained that this becomes "the determining factor as to whether or not you are in the right business. If you're only interested in the economic return, you may need to switch your focus; likewise, if you're only concerned with a social return you may need to switch that, too. Both are important in the impact space," she added. "But you must always remember that people aren't commodities but rather the true value proposition."

Solution #1:

Leadership

Hiring black and brown people is a start but not the solution. You must not become part of the problem! How are the people you want to hire? What's their lived experience? Do you hire Historically Black Colleges and Universities (HBCU) grads or only blacks from white Ivy League schools? I'm always amazed when I'm asked to find a black celebrity or athlete to help support a cause but never a talented black or brown person to join the team.

Every now and then, I'm also asked to identify a black or brown person who would make a good board member. Sadly, they tend to only want the most successful black and brown people—like the white members of the board. But why would successful black and brown people want to join your board and not the ten other homogenous boards with the same story?

Solution #2

Economics

I'm pretty privileged, which sounds funny for me to say, but I've accepted it as true. I opted to work in the sector because I could afford to. While many of my friends were making tons of money, I was making couch money—as it's been called by someone that I'll let remain nameless.

Let's face it, to do this work you sacrifice a lot of material things, and in some cases you can't work in the sector because many people leave college because they have a responsibility to family members.

Not only did I choose a complicated sector, I chose to be an entrepreneur in the sector that is even more complicated that usual. Why? To put it plainly, for the longest time, people thought I should work for free either because the work helps my community or because they doubted that I could produce quality work. Fortunately, not being attached to material things and having some strong allies, I've managed to survive, though it hasn't always been easy.

The point is, most talented black and brown people don't have the luxury of working in and building a practice in a low paying sector dominated by white people who hire their friends first, children, and friends of board members because that's how the social impact sector is set up. The new conversations around diversity and inclusion are still awkward with no real implications for lack of diversity, whereas for-profit corporations tend to face much more scrutiny. It's a lot like what's been known to happen in the tech sector—who is really going to hold their friends accountable?

Solution #3
Reimagine the Sector

There is hope! Last year I attended a TED conference in Vancouver for the first time. At first, I struggled to make sense of it all, but midway through the day, I had an epiphany. It was a space for big ideas. I found a bench to sit on and pulled out a journal and started writing down my big ideas—dreams I had as a child, thoughts about what I once decided could be possible. Then I headed back to the conference for the final talks of the day. That's when it dawned on me that we *can* make this work *if* we cultivate a space for PEOPLE with big ideas to solve complicated problems.

Mitch and Freada Kapor are doing it (at last count they are limited partners in 500 Startups), and my friend James White, Head of Diversity and Inclusion at Oppenheimer Funds, is always serving as an ally, taking risks, and building bridges. My first piece of advice is to find one someone like them and stop trying to convince people who don't get it.

Second, black and brown people have to figure out what's important to them and then go after it. At four years old, I didn't know how to articulate how I felt at that gas station, but I knew that the boy's words were not going to define me. Thankfully, my parents created a world for me that focused on defining me from a place of beauty without negating others. Then I had a foundation on which I continue to base my choices.

For the past six years, I have built a community to help black and brown people reimagine our sector. Anyone who wants to join us understands that we are valuable assets to building a better world.

Christal Jackson creates the kind of unique and thoughtful conversations that truly shape the world for the better. My first experience attending a Head and Heart Philanthropy Summit was not only inspirational, but also challenged my paradigm on how to be as practically committed to diversity goals as I was ideologically. After concluding a talk at the 2015 Summit, a participant essentially said to me, "Your company's diversity goals sound great, but you don't seem like you have a realistic business plan to achieve them." She was right, and it prompted a humbling and honest conversation that transformed my approach and resulted in meaningful changes for my organization.

—Bethany Lampland

7 Simple Solutions to Building Successful Social Impact Models

Solution

#1

Build a Good Reputation (Integrity Counts).

Creating a good reputation is critical to building trust in the community. One key way to build a good relationship is by being inclusive. A sure way to fail or live in total frustration is to build something for people without allowing them to be a part of it. Many well-intended initiatives don't achieve optimal success because they are aimed at "fixing" people rather than equipping and empowering them to "fix" themselves. If you have an idea to help a community, it's a good idea to ask for feedback from the people it will affect. Be sure the idea is culturally sensitive—not only about race, but also about whether it could contradict religious values, norms, and so forth. When you partner with the community you become much more credible than when you dictate to the community.

Solution

#2

Don't Rely on Events—Build Relationships.

All these events are temporary, but relationships are permanent. In this age of social media, it's very tempting to focus on staging the most amazing event with all of the accoutrements. But when the event is over, you might realize you've spent far too much money and not gained any new partners. Yes, gathering is important, but not solely for the sake of gathering. If you have an event, your first metric of success shouldn't be how good the food and beverages were, but how many event attendees you can convert into real relationships. The more conversions to relationships the more donors, stakeholders, and partners you will have. It is essential that you plan, staff, and host events not only to raise funds but also to increase your non-profit's visibility. And once you've planted those seeds of real relationships, be sure to follow-up by building them between events as well. Think of it this way: events might be your sunny, sweet jam, but relationships will always be your bread and butter!

Solution

#3

Have a Clear Mission and Vision.

In this age of perpetual distractions, the concept of mission-planning is highly important. In other words, it's important for you to focus on what you plan to do and what you hope to accomplish. You need to understand *specifically*—in both a written and published form—what your purpose really is, versus just chasing dollars. When you have a clear mission and vision, there are no questions. Your potential partners will know exactly what you stand for, the good works you do, and, if it's done right, exactly where their money will go once they generously donate it. In a world where problems abound, it's tempting to try to solve everything. You can't, and it's okay.

Solution
#4

A Strategic Plan Equals a Solid Business Plan.

This is when you revisit your business roots and get back to the "business of doing good." In other words, review your original plan—the methods you'd devised back in the beginning—and assess how you are doing. Do you need to revamp your budget in order to reflect both lean times and times of terrific bounty? Are you a strategic thinker or are you the ideas person? Strategy work is very different from being process-oriented. The ideas person focuses on concepts: the seeds of good intention. A strategic thinker can take a 30,000-foot view and map out a game plan—in other words, he or she is the one who figures out how to nourish and grow the seeds so they will succeed. I strongly recommend investing in a strategic planning session or acquiring appropriate tools for building your specific strategy.

Solution
#5

Diversify Your Income Streams.

The clearest course toward economic success is one that reminds entrepreneurs not to put all of our financial eggs in a single basket. Diversification isn't just a timely buzzword but a real and aggressive goal that must be considered in order to recession-proof your work. If you have a nonprofit organization, you must have an earned income stream. If your business is for-profit, you must have a stream that generates revenue even when you're sleeping.

Solution # *6*

Scale, Scale, Scale.

Scale: it's the name of the game in big business today. In Silicon Valley, where I live, corporate decision-makers won't even consider taking on something new if it isn't big. Frankly, I don't blame them. When it comes to doing good, go big or don't go. The social problems we face are so complicated that they call for big solutions. If you can replicate your model in a new market, then you are on the right track.

Solution

#7

Have Fun!

No matter what your concept or your goals, if what you are doing doesn't fuel you, then it's time to course correct. The work of social impact is very hard and full of many detours, so you must keep your focus and remember why you started.

Head and Heart Philanthropy Summit was an extraordinary experience. It allowed me to build new relationships while feeling deeply rooted in a shared commitment to social justice. The Vineyard provided the perfect backdrop for the event, with a sense of history, nature, and relaxation that combine to create an atmosphere of positivity and potential. I connected with people from all over the US, and I look forward to seeing those new friendships and partnerships grow.

—Adam Vine

—Section IV—

Onward to Success

Beauty for Ashes

MARTHA'S VINEYARD AND BEYOND: THE SUCCESS OF THIS CURATED COMMUNITY OF LEADERS

Uh oh, I thought as I realized that I had missed a step on a pretty long staircase in the house I'd rented for the week. Both hands were full, and I had a few seconds to figure out my fall. I am a strategist . . . so I released my computer and the other items in my hands, and quickly adjusted my body so I wouldn't hit my head. It was similar to an old move from when I'd been a cheerleader for 13 years long, long ago: I curled a bit so that I wouldn't hit my back. All I could think of was that my head and back were the last two things I wanted to hurt, so after my planning, God dispatched angels to land this fall and *bump bump bump* I went, then finally made it to the landing.

I was hurt. I didn't move for at least a minute. Instead, I tried to figure out how I would get up. The computer looked as if it had survived; the documents, however, had gone flying. But, somehow, I managed to roll a bit onto one side, then I took a deep breath and stood up. I made it to the bathroom where, to my horror, I saw that I was already starting to bruise. In 48 hours the summit that I'd been planning for nearly a year was going to start: the enthusiastic attendees had already arrived on the beautiful island of Martha's Vineyard; my team was also in place to manage logistics, organize registration, design the journal, coordinate ground transportation, and more—which all sounds simple, but when it's show time, and no one is there to supervise, it can turn into a nightmare. So as I stood, staring into the mirror, I had one thought: *I have no one in charge; no one to call to ask them to stand in for me.* I had built a reliable team, but it was about to lose its leader—me. And it was completely my fault.

But first things first. I took a couple of Tylenol, extra-strength, because this was going to hurt and I had no time to stop. Eventually, my mother arrived back at the house. A retired nurse, she took one look at me and said: "Well, it looks like you're likely going to have a hematoma."

She was right. So, thanks to the advice of physician friends, I self-medicated and checked the spot every hour to make certain that it had not moved. Then the summit started and all I could think about was: *How much longer until this will be over?* Each hour that ticked by put me closer to lying down, getting in the hot tub, swimming, and just being quiet. It had been a long journey that I'd been looking forward to so much. But right then, I only felt tired. And incredibly sore.

When I had first conceived this gathering, this meeting of minds and convening to develop good works, it hadn't been to make money, be exclusive, or have a new clique of "cool kids." Instead, I had been tired of hearing people with integrity voice their frustrations about trying to make change throughout our community. Because I had read about Martha's Vineyard and sensed that it was a magical place for black people, I thought: *This is the space.* This was where the ideas about real change could begin to form.

I grew up going to Wharton, Texas, which had been somewhat magical for me. My family had owned land there since 1881, and only our relatives lived on Jackson Lane—with the single exception of a white tenant to whom my grandfather had rented space for many years. Every August we all gathered for Homecoming. One of the relatives preached, and then we ate. After that, we handled the church business for the year, and then did whatever we wanted to do: rode bikes, played games, hung out together. It was a ceremonial place: it was the street where most of us first learned how to drive.

It wasn't long, however, before I realized most black people didn't have a magical place they could retreat to. I wanted to create one. But the dream had been difficult to articulate, tough to express to those I wanted to bring on board.

Early Days

I was very selective about whom to discuss the idea with for a whole host of reasons. Many people immediately directed me to large, white think tanks that were doing this but needed to add some diversity.

For example, I remember some people at Aspen took a phone meeting with me (because someone had asked them to), but I sensed right away that they weren't the least bit interested in figuring out how to bring black people together around this work. For a bit of time, the Aspen group patronized me, but nothing ever happened, for which I'm actually glad.

Then there were corporate folks who thought my concept could be a solid business development opportunity but soon realized that I wasn't interested in getting a few coins in exchange for access to the best and brightest. It felt too much like exploitation to me. I don't believe in exploiting people who have been oppressed long enough.

All the while, I was not worried about how things would work out, because I believed if they should, they would, and if they didn't, then they weren't supposed to. Building this community taught me a lot about myself and other people. The first thing I realized was I didn't love money enough. I soon knew that the reason I couldn't build a reliable team was because too many people were focused on monetizing the work. I was not. I've never led with money; I don't worry about money.

I believe we can earn more money than we could ever spend, so I worried about other things, like:

- Will this be the right mix of people?
- Will I have the right expert for a topic?
- Will the summit attendees be able to leave with new connections to further their work?

I never worried if the sign was cute enough, if we had enough banners, or if everyone would like the outfit I wore. Instead, I focused on whether the attendees would leave with the knowledge they'd need to really do the work. Perhaps, I don't worry about money because all of my life everything I've needed, I had, and I also had most of what I wanted. I think, because of that, I tend to attract abundance, but, unfortunately, that attracts opportunists, too.

Figuring It Out . . .

It wasn't long before I realized that my concept was totally viable, and what I had hoped would happen for people, was, in fact, happening. From that very first summit and onward, I saw everyone making connections, getting funding and learning.

Around year three, I integrated the roster of speakers. That was also when I learned some valuable advice about the business of convening from a source who was as committed as I was to seeing change in the world and to creating models of sustainability, both of which are mutually important. I had grown weary of people making money off the pain of black and brown people. That is so much of what the social impact sector is at the core, creating programs and policies that they profit from in the name of helping poor black and brown kids. After I attended yet another very important event where a group raised a ton of money, employed white people in all of the senior leadership roles, gave a few black and brown people jobs to serve on the frontline, I remember saying to myself, *Lord I don't want to go to another one of these things. I've had enough.* Right then and there, I promised myself to make certain I wouldn't have to sit in those rooms to sustain my work. Thankfully, I haven't.

But much like my inability to build a reliable team because people tended to think I pocketed lots of money and they wouldn't get any, I did not know how to prove that simply wasn't true, because I give over half of what I raise away. I had hoped to build a pipeline for millennials to learn and to use my model as an opportunity to access what they would need to grow and thrive. That didn't happen and it's fine, because what did happen was that emerging leaders found a space where they could be expertly counseled, stretched beyond their dreams and expectations, and connected to people and organizations that could help bring their hard work to fruition. What did happen was that senior leaders shared their wisdom, and, in turn, built their legacy. Suddenly, entrepreneurs and investors could connect, identify resources, and scale—all under the auspices of a new framework, through a new lens, based on a foundation of people of color as their primary assets.

The Asset Challenge

I'm convinced that when my great great-grandfather, Arthur Jackson Sr., worked to buy land for his children and their descendants 133 years ago, it wasn't easy. A harsh racial climate, coupled with disbelief from his own uncertainty about if he could keep it once he got it, likely filled his mind. But he did it because he recognized the value of assets and that land offered a substantial one. Long before my parents were born and met, he was planning for their future because he believed they would be worth it.

Like my great great-grandfather's investment, the intentionality of the work must be focused on something beyond the moment, beyond the who can "I" meet to help "me" with "my project." Rather the goal must be on what you are building for those coming behind you. Truth be told, today most everyone has enough stuff, and most of what we have we don't know what to do with it. I've been guilty of that, too, but I wanted to be better. So I mapped my assets and set a new course to be more thoughtful about the work I do. I'm committed to building partnerships with those who share the same values. That way, I know if I fall down the stairs again (though I pray that doesn't happen), I will have someone I can call who truly will be willing and able to help.

Thanks to the advice of my expert impact-convener, I have trimmed my contact list and adjusted the point of entry so that every person on it reflects the value of the experience, but more importantly, the value of my assets—people.

Now it's your turn to get started on the most fulfilling journey of your lifetime!

Models of Impact

Charles Johnson Foundation

IMPACTING RURAL COMMUNITIES

A native of Hawkinsville, Georgia, this Carolina Panthers Defensive End made the decision to do for his hometown what he longed for others to do: give back. Raised by a single mother, Mr. Johnson had the values of hard work and integrity deeply ingrained in him at an early age. Growing up in poverty didn't make Charles bitter—it made him determined. With an unusually long career in the NFL, he made his dream of giving back a reality by launching a foundation and awarding scholarships to first generation college students who excel in both sports and academics. His first investment was in scholarships. Each year he awards four students a $5,000 scholarship and renews the award throughout their four years in school. To date, he has contributed over $320,000 in academic scholarships, and he also hosts an annual Sports and Academic Camp. As the sole underwriter, each summer he has hosted nearly 1,500 youth, introducing them to world-class athletes, STEM education activities, and new sports apparel. At first glance, sports camps might not seem to be unique, but in rural America they are a big deal by serving to remind persons from underserved rural communities that a gesture of kindness makes young people who are otherwise not connected to other parts of the world feel connected. Johnson's investment in Hawkinsville will shift the trajectory of generations to come by offering resources and time.

GirlTrek

HEALTH AMBASSADORS

When Vanessa Garrison and T. Morgan Dixon set out to provide education about preventable health issues, they found tremendous success by reminding black women about the health benefits of walking just thirty minutes a day. Sounds simple: well yes, and no. Today they have nearly 16K Twitter followers, and women are walking, reclaiming their communities, health, and self-confidence. This simple act of taking a walk has turned into a glorious celebration of self-care and has renewed the importance of community among black women. GirlTrek is rapidly becoming synonymous with the names of longstanding civic organizations that have been focused on serving women for decades. No doubt the benefits of modern technology have helped this organization grow and will help it continue to grow. Together, Ms. Garrison and Ms. Dixon took an idea, married it with technology, and are now leading health ambassadors. Neither woman was from enormous wealth—in fact, they met at work: ordinary women with a vision and with a passion to see it through. The impact they have created to change women's lives for the better will be felt for generations. From weight loss, to overcoming depression, to social activism, a myriad of uplifting stories are echoed throughout their success. Whoever thought a walking group could create such long-term seeds of change?

Neighborhood Start Fund

POVERTY DISRUPTORS

It was a Sunday night a restaurant in Palo Alto, California my dear friend, Ana Lewis told me I needed to attend a dinner to see what this woman and her fellow partner were building. I'm always game to meet people who believe in doing hard work and no doubt what Di-Ann Eisnor and Lupe Fiasco are two of the bravest souls I've encountered in a while. You see Di-Ann, founder of Waze, could have easily disappeared after her success into the world of tech privilege but instead she dug in to tackle one of the biggest challenges facing this country bridging the gap between the have and have nots but not by being charitable but by literally finding and investing in the next version of herself. What many don't know is that she like the people she invests in are a lot like her, underserved and overlooked. Long before her days as in Silicon Valley, she was a poor ordinary girl from a family of truck drivers. Now one of the most powerful women in tech, her genius and compassion make her a force. Her background and success coupled with the sheer genius of Lupe Fiasco makes for an unparalleled duo, together they will single-handedly lift generations out of poverty and shift the trajectory of their lives for generations by investing in entrepreneurs. Lupe understands the challenges of urban America but as a social architect he also understands real change happens at a systemic level. Lupe is more than a rapper; he's a linguist who distinctly understands the interplay between sound and meaning.

Therefore, with a hyper local approach of creating economic impact in underserved neighborhoods this means more diverse entrepreneurs are connected to the possibility to build wealth and improve the neighborhoods where they reside.

Kapor Center for Social Impact

The names Mitch Kapor and Freada Kapor Klein are synonymous with tech and impact investing. Based in Oakland, California, they have invested more than any venture capitalists in black and brown ventures. As bold leaders they have challenged the status quo in Silicon Valley and beyond. They are foremost leaders in social justice by continuing to improve economic outcomes that will shift the economic reality for many families for multiple generations. As successful business leaders, they took their expertise and applied it to social issues that plague many black and brown entrepreneurs: a lack of access to capital. At the phase when many are able to turn to their friends and family for seed investment, Mitch and Freada become early investors for those who have no one to turn to. They typically act as the "friends and family" for many concepts and innovations that otherwise would not have been funded. In addition, they have a unique understanding of what it means to be an impact investor: they believe that investing should become "gap-closing." In other words, if an idea does not alleviate the harm being done to the poor or the disadvantaged, then it's not a good idea. Sounds pretty simple, but in capitalistic society negative impact—or no impact—happens far too often. Through the Kapor Center for Social Impact, they are able to dispel several myths —including the one claiming that investing to solve a social problem isn't profitable.

What do all of the Models of Impact have in common, and what can you learn from them?

Your lived experience equips you to follow the examples of these leaders. Following are three steps they did to achieve success—steps you, too, should take as you move forward toward reaching your own goals:

1) **They solved a problem**. They asked themselves what issue or issues were presenting a huge barrier to their success or happiness. They knew it was likely an issue that was shared by others. Then they focused on determining how they thought it could be fixed or prevented. What about your project? Following their methods is a good place to start.

2) **They implemented a process**. They asked themselves what steps were required to fix this problem. You might want to make a journal in which you include practical things that you do on a regular basis around how to prevent or solve this problem.

3) **They determined the scale for their business**. What about you: can you sell your business? Years ago I participated in a YPO accelerator, and that was one of the first questions we were asked. If you have built something that you can sell then you can definitely scale the business . . . an essential step toward success.

Who knew that three days on the Vineyard could lead to new partnerships, new funding opportunities and new friendships? By participating as a 2016 cohort member, I learned that this is the magic of the Head and Heart Philanthropy Summit. Not only is my organization stronger thanks to a new funding partnership with a national organization that I met while on the Vineyard, but I am a stronger leader due to the relationships (turned friendships) that I have developed with thought leaders from diverse backgrounds offering different perspectives and ideas.

—Aisha Nyandoro

—Section V—

The Final Word

Each Piece of Every Mosaic Carries the Spirit of Its Own Story

CHOOSING FREEDOM: MY GIRLTREK STORY
REV. DR. THERESA S. THAMES, PRINCETON, NJ

It's a vicious cycle. A cycle that I learned at a very young age growing up in Southern Mississippi. If you are hungry: eat. It you're tired: eat. If there is a reason to celebrate: eat. If you are sad and depressed: eat. I learned that life revolves around feelings and food. Thus, I had come to believe that food was the balm to soothe all of the issues of my heart and soul. Unfortunately, I was enslaved in the vicious cycle of feeling and eating with no way to break free.

By the time I was fourteen years old, I weighed 280 pounds. By the time I was thirty-three years old, I was 447 pounds. Nevertheless, I carried my weight with pride and always made sure that I was stylishly dressed. I flippantly blamed my southern roots and "big bones" for my voluptuous size. However, the truth was that I was trapped in the vicious cycle and had mastered the art of feeling and eating. If I were to be completely honest, I was not happy. I was miserable, afraid, depressed, and dying. I had eaten my way through an abusive marriage, a demanding career, an emotional divorce, the death of my sister, the death of my father, the death of my ex-husband, years of grief, and the realities of single motherhood. I was literally eating my life away.

A glimpse of freedom came into my life when I mistakenly landed on the Facebook page of **GirlTrek: Healthy Black Women and Girls**. This page showed images of smiling black women taking charge of their health through walking. I "liked" the page and read the posts. I then entered a simple competition and won a t-shirt. The winning t-shirt was not happenstance, but a divine connection and intervention. One of the founders of GirlTrek, Vanessa Garrison, e-mailed me and asked me to join the movement. GirlTrek saved my life.

Unbeknownst to them, they asked me to pray for the #iAmHarriet National GirlTrek gathering when I was in the midst of fighting my way through darkness and depression. The message of GirlTrek was not, "Hey, you fat black woman, work out to lose weight and get thin." The words that the founders Vanessa and Morgan spoke were, "Walk yourself to FREEDOM." They did not ask me to record my food intake or count my steps. They simply said, "Sister, we love you. We believe in you. We need you to love yourself enough to commit to walking thirty minutes a day." THIS I could do. THIS I could commit to. On Sunday, March 10, 2013, I chose freedom.

As GirlTrek celebrates the life and legacy of Harriet Tubman, I, too, celebrate my freedom. GirlTrek and Mother Harriet have taught me that freedom of spirit, mind, and body is possible now in this earthen vessel. I learned to walk and pray. I learned to walk and surrender. I learned to walk and listen to God's great dream for my life. I walked my way to freedom from depression, stress, and that vicious cycle. I walked and walked until 250 pounds of burdens lifted from my body. In choosing freedom, I walked into the fullness of God's love, grace, and power. However, my freedom and healing are not enough.

Harriet Tubman once said, "I freed a thousand slaves. I could have freed a thousand more if only they knew they were slaves." When I trek and work out in my GirlTrek gear, I am making a statement and declaring a mission to model healing, health, self-care, and freedom to women and girls who look like me. GirlTrek is a beautiful sister full of hope in the midst of despair, joy in the midst of pain, and love in a world of hate. Join the sisterhood. Get a taste of freedom forever changed. Get free.

Cozumel, Mexico

JANUARY 14, 2016

In the summer of 1998, I received an e-mail from my academic advisor telling me that my Masters thesis had been rejected. In that instant, all my plans were thrown out of whack. I was in Washington, DC doing an internship with the Children's Defense Fund as part of the National Capitol Semester for Seminarians, and I had just interviewed with Congresswoman Sheila Jackson Lee. I was preparing to purchase my first home in the city, and I was exhaling because I could finally be done with this field of study and divinity school. I felt that my career was finally beginning.

And suddenly, there was the e-mail. Even today, I remember the startling back-and-forth communication that followed with my advisor as plainly as if it took place yesterday. I also know that after I tried to digest her reasoning, I was livid, on the edge of a temper tantrum: I just sat on the floor of my apartment, too angry to cry. I called a couple of people, but they didn't know what to say, so their answers sounded as crazy as my thoughts.

I decided to take a walk around the city and try to cool off. The shady residential neighborhoods with their picturesque red brick streets had always felt familiar to me. And very safe. It was a place where I knew could feel centered.

A couple of years earlier, when I'd been an undergraduate student in Atlanta, my college president, Johnetta B. Cole, had asked us about our summer plans. At the time, I wasn't sure about mine. Somehow our conversation ended up to be about the African Burial Grounds Project, and it resonated with me. The only problem was, in order to be part of the project I would have to spend the summer in Washington, DC. Immediately, I started researching housing options, and found space on the campus of Georgetown University. Though the room was in what was likely the oldest dorm on the campus, it served its purpose. Because I love libraries, one day I wandered into the one at the university to read. Of course, I remember very little, except that it was a delightful distraction. I knew I loved the Georgetown environment; for some reason, I felt connected to it and to all the possibilities it opened for me. Then one day I learned that the brick streets of the city had been built by slaves. My ancestors. My people. No wonder I felt that I belonged there. And felt safe.

Fast-forward to the day I learned about the demise of my Masters thesis. As I walked around Washington, I found myself back in Georgetown on the university campus. It was almost as if my ancestors had guided me there, had helped me search for clarity in the chaos that was whirling in my mind. Continuing to ponder my advisor's words, I slowly began to feel my anger settle. I returned to my apartment and re-read the initial e-mail. That's when it started to sink in that because my thesis had been rejected, I would have to stay in school another semester. Normally this would not have devastated me, because even back then I knew how to tackle adversity. But I absolutely *hated* seminary, and I felt that if I had to go back to Durham, I would just die. I racked my brain trying to come up with a solution, including how things might work if I transferred to another school. Of course, I kept berating myself, telling myself I should have gone to Princeton when they'd offered me the chance, that I wouldn't be in this mess if I had. I was miserable, sad, confused; I felt as if I were being punished for hating seminary.

Then I became determined to turn this around. So instead of continuing to mope, I went back to the university library and did some research. That's when I discovered that Georgetown had a religious studies program. I started to think that if I could transfer my credits, then maybe I could be done with this instead of having to write a new thesis or rewrite the original one, which I knew I was not going to do. Without hesitation, I made my way to an admissions counselor—and quickly found myself enrolling in a summer program to study abroad in Italy. It seemed like a terrific place to start exploring other options.

I notified the congresswoman's office that I needed to withdraw my application for the position. Then, with no apprehension—though still a bit foggy about what would come next—I found myself in Florence, Italy, studying religious art. And I became intrigued by mosaics.

Armed with a notebook and pen, I spent hours writing down my thoughts while studying each one. The work was incredibly fulfilling. When I wasn't studying, I roamed the streets freely at dusk, I journaled religiously, and I allowed myself to get lost in all the rich beauty all around me. It was literally and figuratively a long way from the floor in my apartment where I had sat, feeling nothing but the anger of rejection.

On one of my last days in Florence, Italy, I decided to celebrate my twenty-fourth birthday by having a hand-drawn picture of me done by an incredible artist who sat in the plaza with his easel. When I saw the finished piece, I gasped. Staring back at me was not only my own image, but also the image of my grandmother Georgia Elizabeth (Eggleston) Walker. I took that as immense reassurance that regardless of where I wound up in life, the presence of my ancestors would always be there to guide me. My grandmother Walker had passed before I'd been born; I only knew her through stories that had been passed down and shared, and through the beautiful picture that hung on the wall in my aunt's living room in Port Gibson, Mississippi.

In Italy, I fell in love with mosaics. They were beautiful, messy, bold, captivating, mysterious, and undeniable—all while being fragile. To me, they were like real-time images holding that moment in time, a moment that could neither be imitated nor redone. They were perfectly imperfect—a lot like my journey and me. I imagined that each piece of a mosaic originated from something else at one point in time, but that it had gone through a process to become a part of a larger puzzle.

Have you ever noticed how all the pieces of a mosaic are small remnants, small parts of something else? Isn't that the same as us human beings? We all come from somewhere, but we've been carefully carved and shaped from our point of origin. The making of a mosaic seems to correlate to a three-step process of life. First, each part is broken, chipped away, recreated from its original state. This can happen any number of ways: I imagine that the stone is dropped or beaten, leaving the fragments. Next, the pieces are arranged—carefully, painstakingly, by the hands of the artist. The final step is when the completed piece is shared with the world, the same way that we are. When I had been studying African-American literature at Spelman College, I remember that I often became lost in the pages of some amazing books, only to discover who I was becoming. One day, one of my professors walked into the classroom and asked us: "Do you want to be well?" I remember thinking: "I'm not sick." In fact we all started saying that we felt fine, we were not sick. Then the professor introduced us to Toni Cade Bambara's novel, *The Salt Eaters*, which had won the American Book Award in 1980. I revisited that book while absorbing the beautiful gardens in Italy, while bereft on the floor in my apartment, and while wandering the streets of Georgetown that my slave ancestors had built. But now the time had come for me to grow up, which, like the pieces of the mosaic, I knew meant that I had been broken and thrown off course. Having been named the Most Outstanding Student in my high school class, having graduated with over a 4.0, and having attained perfect attendance throughout my high school years, I had gone on to Spelman, the only school I had applied to. When my thesis was rejected, I could not believe—I could not accept—that rejection was possible. Not for me.

Once I got over myself and accepted that, for some reason, this time I had not succeeded, I started to rewrite my thesis. I also began to work as a substitute teacher. The more I did, the more I learned about the nonprofit sector. Soon, I became a student of the field. None of that might have happened had I not experienced the crush of failure, enrolled at Georgetown, gone to Italy, and found life's "bigger picture" through the beautiful mosaics.

As was my habit, I read anything that I could get my hands on in order to understand the science and operation of the nonprofit sector. The sector spoke to me because I saw that in some ways it offered the cure to what had ailed me most about church: I had come to view the church as merely an organization or a business framed around scripture. On the other hand, I felt that the nonprofit sector presented an entire field dedicated to helping those who often could not help themselves.

It wasn't long before I forgot how unhappy I'd been about the rejected thesis, because I had discovered a new career path to helping people. Before then, no one could have told me that I would end up leading a social impact agency focused on improving education, health, and economic outcomes for communities of color. When I'd been a second year seminarian, I had no idea that this world even existed. My grandmother, who had died prematurely because blacks could not receive the same healthcare as whites, could never have imagined some of the places I have traveled, advocating for people like herself, people who were discriminated against due to their race. The young woman who had wandered around Georgetown feeling lost and alone, had actually been having her life re-arranged so that she would one day be able to help others put together the pieces of their own journey as they worked toward achieving wholeness and purpose.

The question posed by my professor years ago, "Do you want to be well?" has grown to have new meaning for me. My answer is now a definitive *Yes*, because my wellness is inextricably linked to the wellness and advancement of others.

After all, each of us is an important part of the mosaic of life. And we all bring with us the steps of those who have come and gone before us.

Epilogue

Before I was 10 years old, I suffered two serious injuries to my face that would affect me forever. Although they were not visible to most, I saw the effects every morning when I washed my face, looked in the mirror, and then again when I washed my face before bed. I saw them at the hair salon and at doctor appointments. There were no signs on the outside but I felt the impact of these two nearly fatal falls every day.

My history with these falls is the story of humanity, as all of us are broken and doing our best to keep it together. And it's because of our brokenness that we are similar. I have come to believe that broken pieces can create beautiful things, mosaics.

Years ago at an AME General Conference I heard a sermon by Bishop John R. Bryant that I will always remember. He described the process that God takes us through in order to live the life that we were created for. First, God creates us, and we become broken. Life happens and we are given away. Then, we are sent into the world to fulfill our life mission.

When I see people doing good in the world, I see a mosaic, broken pieces making beautiful things.

www.ingramcontent.com/pod-product-compliance
Lightning Source LLC
Chambersburg PA
CBHW021624270326
41931CB00008B/855